Out-O

CROSSWORDS

By Betty Greene

Watermill Press

How to use the picture clues in these crossword puzzles:
Some of the clues in these puzzles are picture clues. Use them to fill in parts of the puzzles. An **A** label on a picture clue stands for **Across,** and a **D** label stands for **Down.** For example, if a picture clue has the label **16D,** it means the word that correctly describes the picture is the answer to **16 Down** in the puzzle diagram. A label of **8A** would mean that the description of the picture clue is the answer to **8 Across** in the puzzle diagram.

Cover design and illustration by Rod L. Gonzalez

Printed in the United States of America.

10 9 8 7 6 5 4 3 2 1

Something Easy

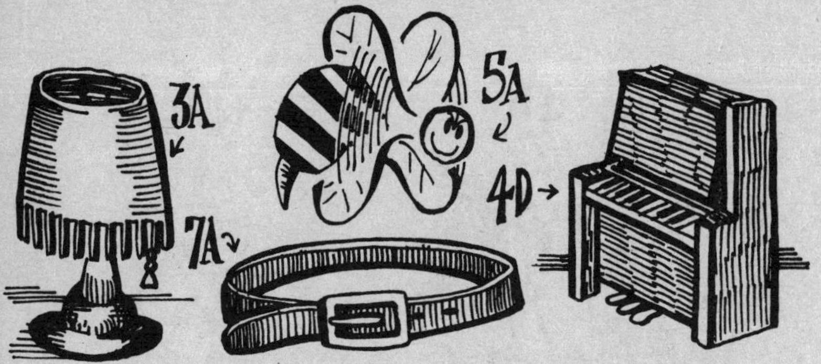

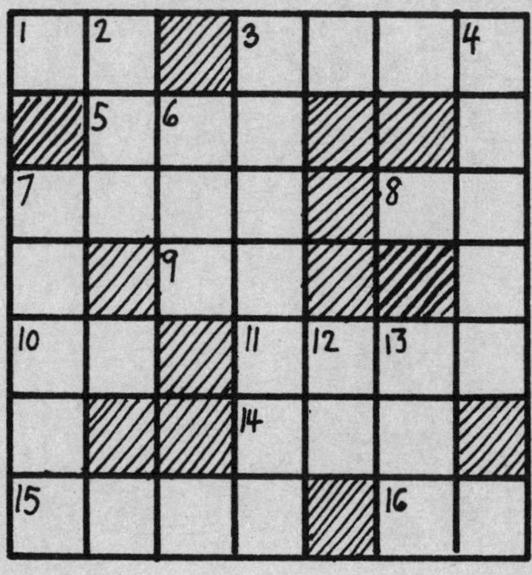

ACROSS

1. Mother.
8. Father.
9. That thing.
10. Musical note.
11. "Do ______ others . . ."
14. Sound a pigeon makes.
15. There's no place like ________.
16. Myself.

DOWN

2. Lincoln's first name.
3. A green vegetable.
6. ____ Whitney invented the cotton gin.
7. A tree with white bark.
12. Not yes.
13. Male turkey or cat.

A Warm-Up

ACROSS

1. Big tops; shows in a big tent.
4. Inquires.
7. Found on a witch's nose or chin.
8. Snakelike fish.
9. "_____ the king's horses and _____ the king's men..."

DOWN

2. Lions do this.
3. Happy grin.
5. The North ____ is the brightest one of all.
6. "I'd rather do it my__ __ __ __."
10. 51: Roman numerals.

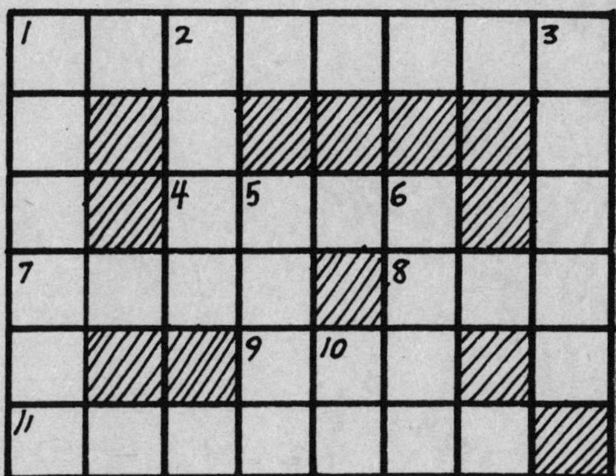

Fun With Pictures

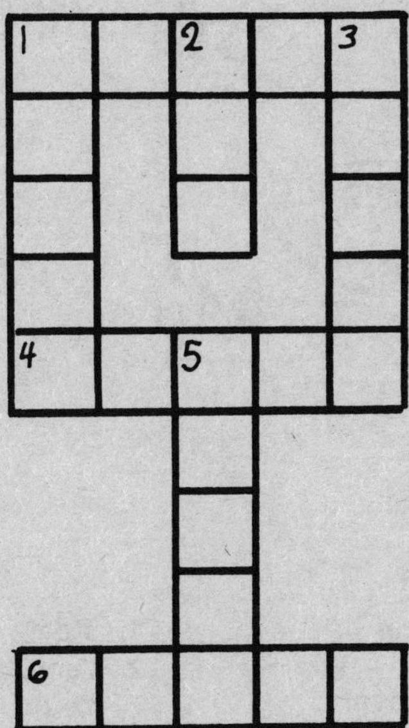

Having A Ball!

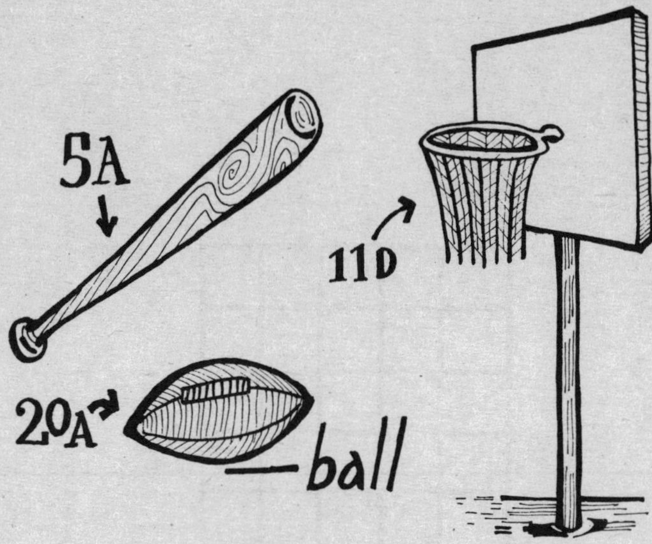

ACROSS

3. Game played on horseback.
9. Add up; final count.
11. You get to first _____ on a single.
13. Not many.
14. Each one has five fingers.
15. Game played with a net and rackets.
17. A large ball you hit with your hands.
21. Northwest: Abbr.

DOWN

1. Steal.
2. Very warm.
4. Musical note.
6. _ _ _ _ball; opposite of hard.
7. Young deer.
8. Person who sits in the stands and cheers.
10. Place for a golf ball.
12. South Dakota: Abbr.
14. Short, friendly greeting.
16. Synthetic fabric.
18. Home ___ the brave.
19. ____ ball; below the knees in baseball.

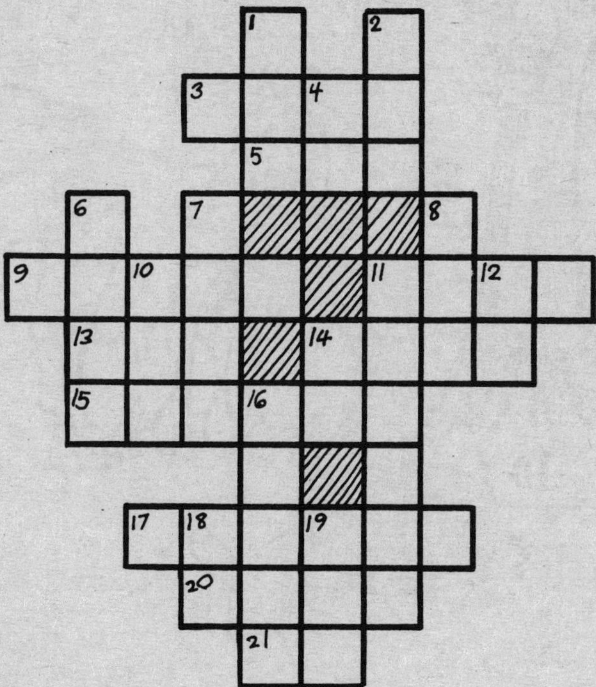

Short and Sweet

ACROSS

4. Unusual.
6. All right.
7. Junior: Abbr.
8. Exist.
9. Enemy.
11. The fur around a lion's head.

DOWN

2. Either.
3. You and I.
4. Steal.
7. Funny story.
9. To keep you cool.
10. Sun God of ancient Egypt.

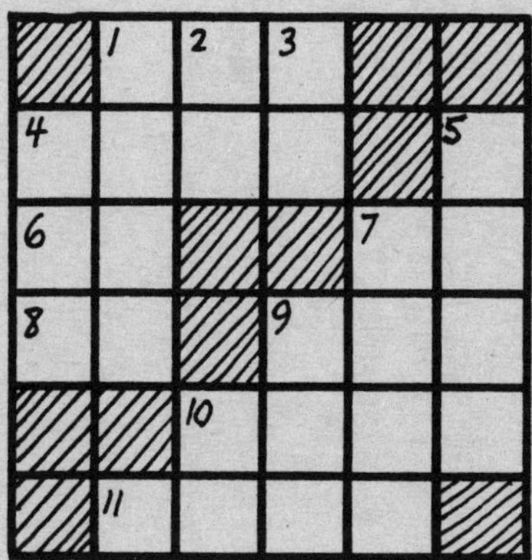
1
2
3
4
5
6
7
8
9
10
11

Be My Valentine

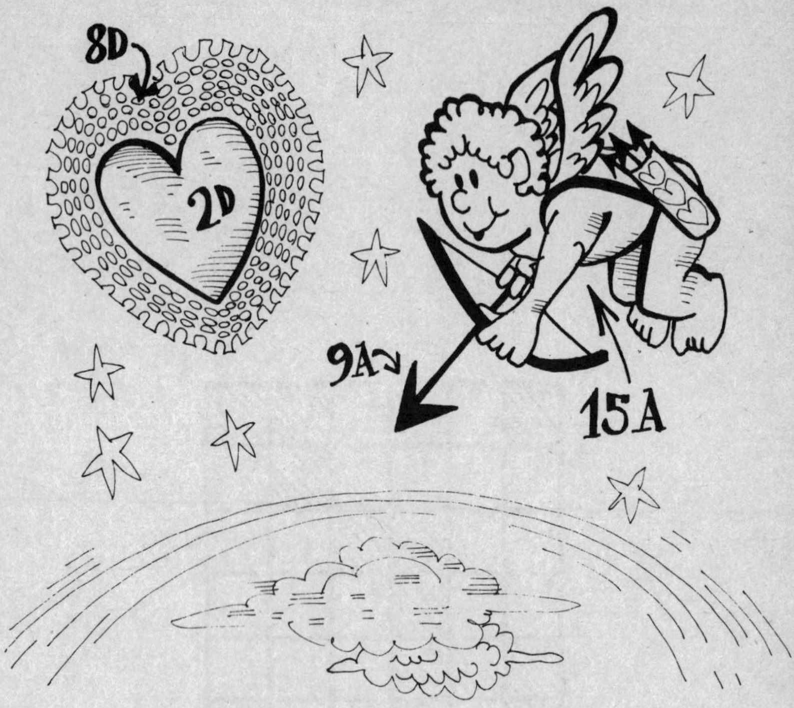

ACROSS

2. Opposite of villain.
3. Less than one; nothing.
5. Ancient Peruvian Indian.
11. Word that is a sigh.
13. Insect that loves picnics.
14. Virginia; Abbr.
16. She lays eggs.
17. For example: Abbr.
18. Belonging to me.

DOWN

1. Happy smile.
4. On top of.
6. A sweet gift.
7. Valentine's day is when you say "I ______ you!"
10. Dwindle; fade.
12. A way to show affection.
13. Point a gun at a target.

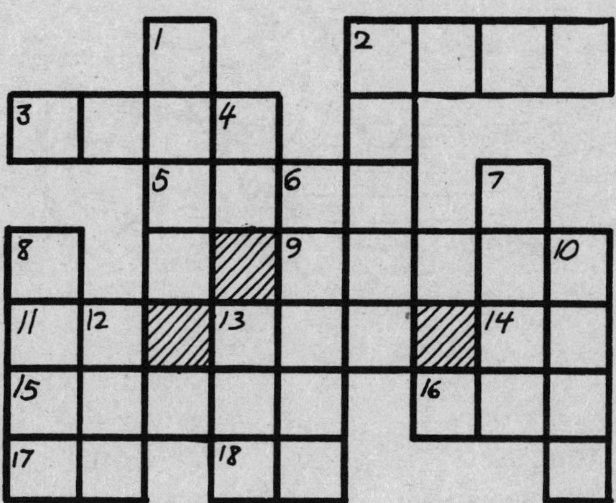

Campsite

ACROSS

1. 4th note in the musical scale.
3. River in Egypt.
4. Not less.
5. Ghost word.
6. Example: Abbr.
7. Wonder and respect.
9. Between-meal treat.
12. Relative.
14. Not wet.
17. Finish.

DOWN

2. Boy's name.
3. Opposite of yes.
5. Homonym for bee.
8. Cool drink for hikes.
9. Two points on a compass.
13. Light brown color.
16. Road: Abbr.

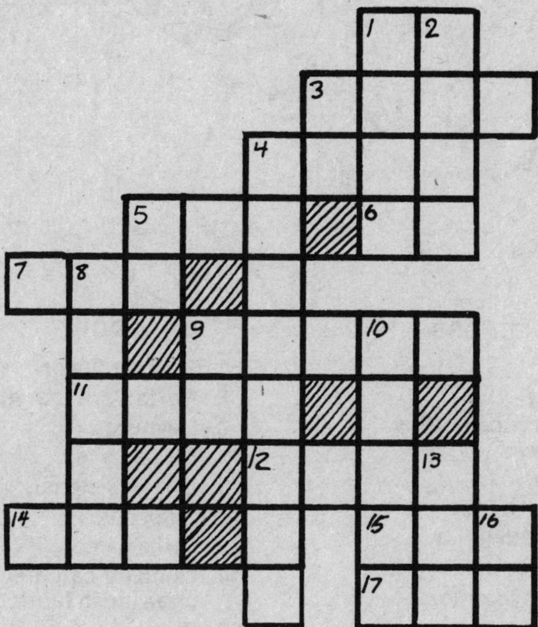
1
2
3
4
5
6
7
8
9
10
11
12
13
14
15
16
17

Sweets for the Sweet

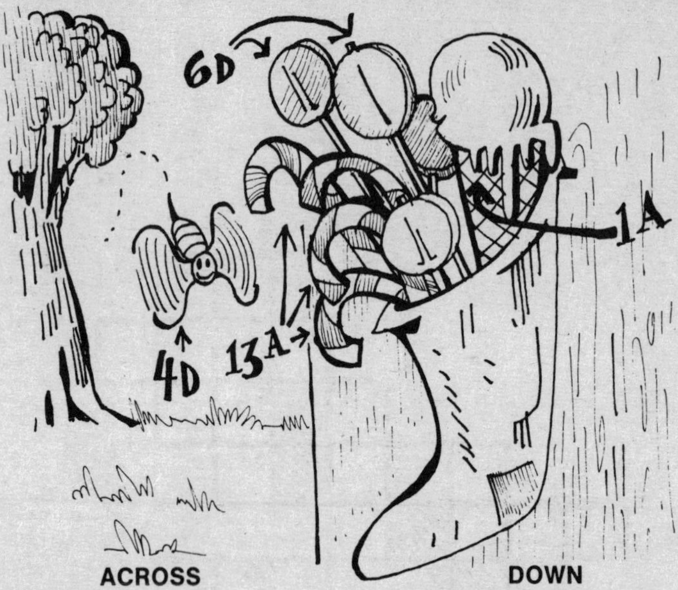

ACROSS

4. Sour ______; hard candy.
7. What soda bottles come in.
9. Upon.
11. Part of a foot.
12. The 12th letter.
15. Everybody.
16. Sign of danger.
17. Friend.
18. Allow.
19. Nap; doze.
20. Like.
21. Spot; mark.
22. Negative answer.
23. One who poses.
25. 2, 4, and 6 are _____ numbers.
26. Spoils, like fruit.

DOWN

1. Popular flavor.
2. North Carolina: Abbr.
3. Devoured.
5. Sly ___ a fox.
8. Distress signal.
10. Titles; nick_ _ _ _ _.
12. Girl's name.
14. Good for catching fish; open mesh fabric.
15. Ginger _ _ _.
17. Change slightly.
19. Squares of grass-covered earth.
21. Boy's name.
23. Myself.
24. ___ and behold!

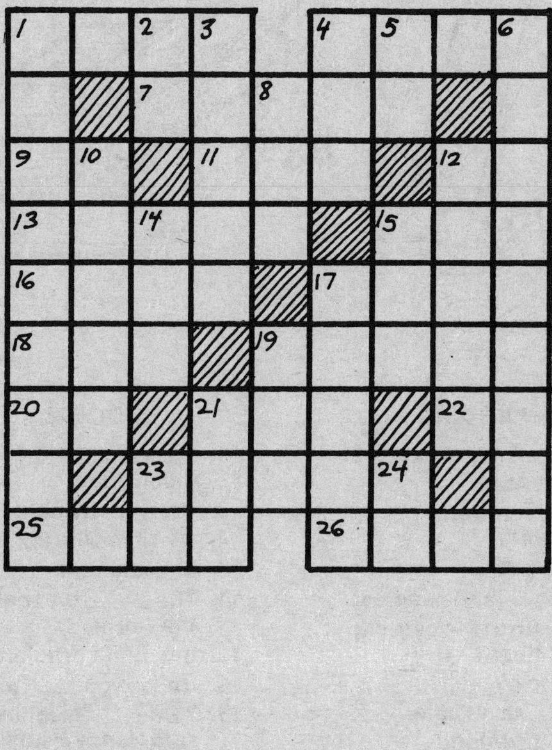
1
2
3
4
5
6
7
8
9
10
11
12
13
14
15
16
17
18
19
20
21
22
23
24
25
26

Head of the Class

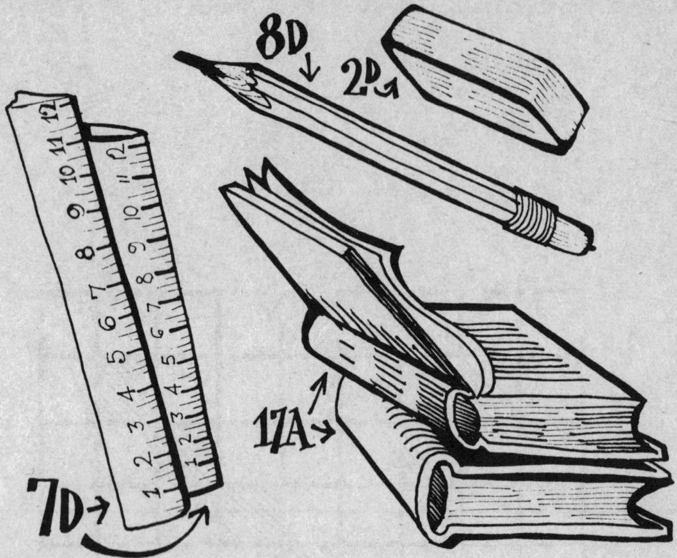

ACROSS

2. Run off to get married.
4. Pair: Abbr.
5. "___ market, ___ market . . ."
6. Instructor.
8. On ____ and needles.
9. Cousin of the ostrich; flightless bird.
10. Close by.
13. I ____ do it; able.
15. Senior: Abbr.
16. Evergreen tree.
19. Everyone.
20. ____ one; single.
21. What you sleep on.

DOWN

1. Fuss and ______; much ado.
3. Story in rhyme.
4. It writes with ink.
6. Musical note.
11. The _____ bird catches the worm.
12. Indefinite article.
14. Solitary; a ____ wolf.
15. "The ____ is falling!" said Henny Penny.
16. Musical note.
17. _ _ _sled.
18. Antique; ancient.

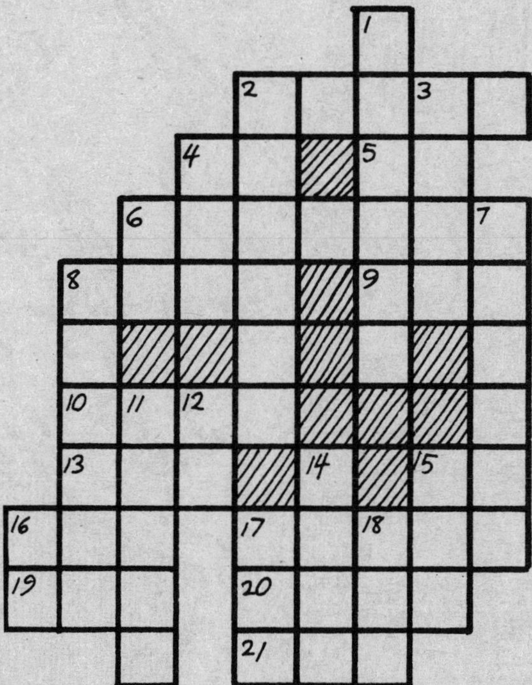

Music, Maestro!

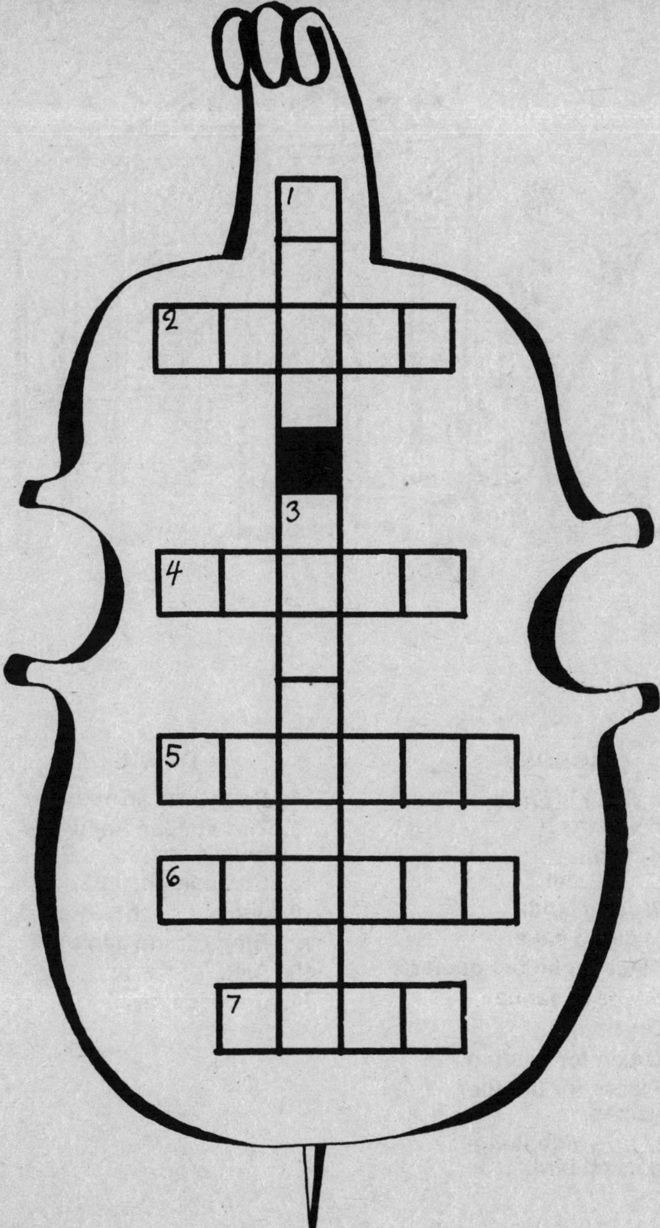
1
2
3
4
5
6
7

Hop, Skip and Jump

ACROSS

1. A sister in *Little Women.*
4. Kanga__ __ __; __ __ __ster.
5. Writing fluid.
6. Makes a cake.
9. Place for indoor games.
10. A type of dance.
11. Dry mud.
13. Organ for hearing.
15. Places for outdoor games.
16. __ __ __rich; long-necked bird.

DOWN

1. Song from an opera.
3. The wooden frame that joins oxen.
8. Companion; pal.
10. Jump ____; heavy cord.
12. Ring ____ (a game).
13. Self.
14. Spoil; decay.

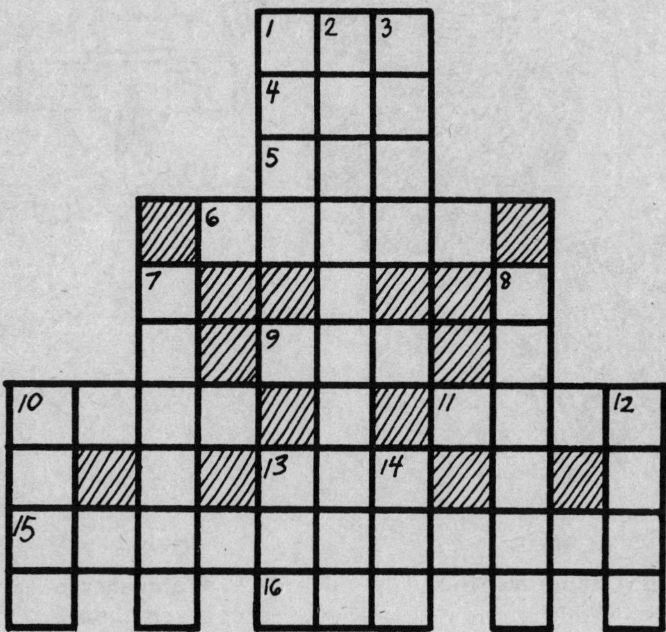
1
2
3
4
5
6
7
8
9
10
11
12
13
14
15
16

Americana

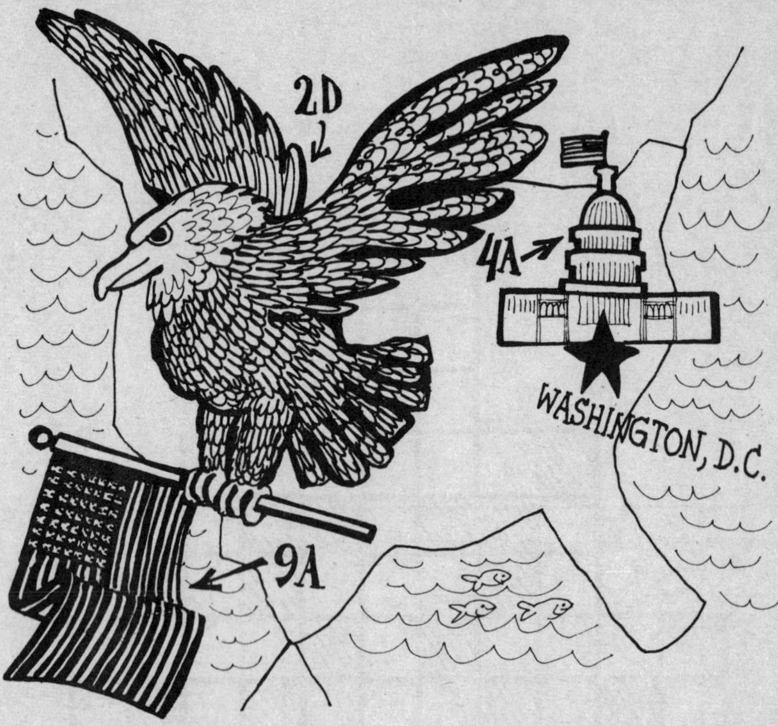

ACROSS

7. Abe Lincoln lived in a ____ cabin.
8. President after Lyndon Johnson.
10. Outdoor restaurant.
12. Made from beets or cane.
16. "____ nation, indivisible . . ."
17. Mail.
18. Daily food and drink.
19. Desire.

DOWN

1. To fly an airplane alone.
3. Finger decorations.
4. Popular American beverage.
5. Musical note.
6. It's in the air we breathe.
10. Cape ____.
11. Black cuckoo bird.
13. United States of America: Abbr.
14. Insect.
15. Road: Abbr.

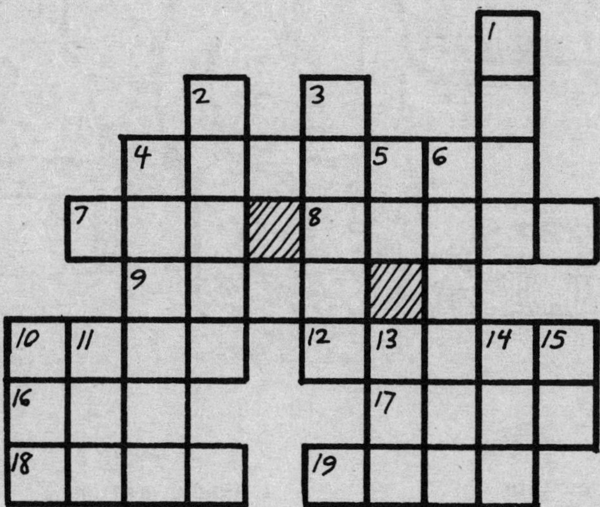

Bake Shop

ACROSS

4. Room: Abbr.
6. Push; shove.
8. ____ and pepper; seasoning.
9. Have breakfast or lunch.
10. Leg joint.
11. Delaware: Abbr.
13. Cravat.
14. Torn bit of cloth.

DOWN

1. He crows at dawn.
3. Yard: Abbr.
4. Small, round bread.
5. Small hotel, usually on a highway.
8. Cut with scissors.
10. Word found in *flat*.
12. Part of you that disappears when you stand up.

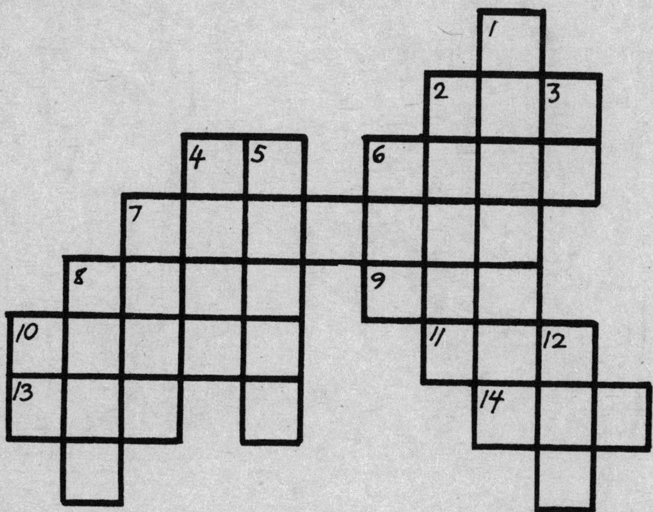

The First Thanksgiving

ACROSS

2. _______ Rock; where the Pilgrims landed.
6. Home for a bee.
7. Shade of purple; name of a flower.
8. Good for winter skating.
10. Angel's headdress.
17. Captain _ _ _ _ of "20,000 Leagues Under the Sea."
19. Professional: short form.
20. Baste, hem or embroider.

DOWN

1. Front _______; place to sit in the summertime.
3. 56: Roman numerals.
4. Shouted.
5. A dog wags it.
12. Found in a shoe lace, or in tangled hair.
13. Shrill barks.
15. Rhymes with star.
16. Not later.
18. Past tense ending.

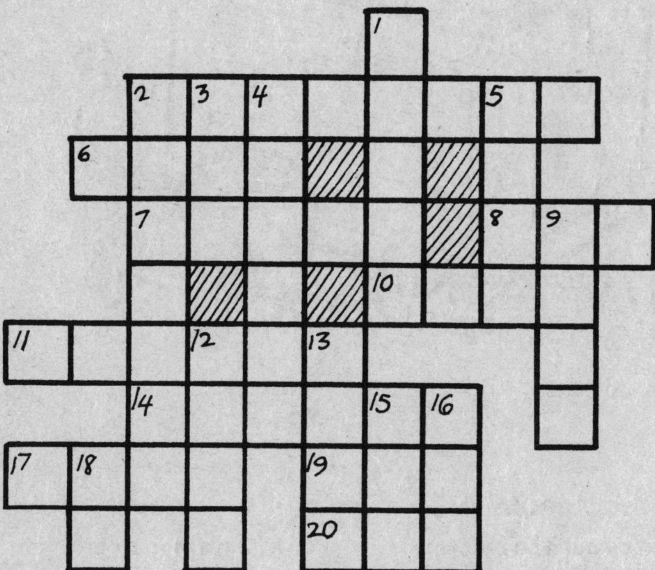

Toy Chest

ACROSS

2. You put it on before your shoe.
6. Boy's name in Russia.
9. What you jump with.
12. Large white animal that lives at the North Pole.
13. With permission," ___ your leave."
14. Rhymes with fat cat.
15. Garden tool.
19. Enormous.
20. Climbing plant.

DOWN

1. Governor: Abbr.
2. Foolish.
4. Door handle.
8. Part of the ear.
10. The top of a mountain.
11. Dine.
16. The Wizard of ___.
17. Month.
18. Civil Engineer: Abbr.
19. A friendly way to say hello.

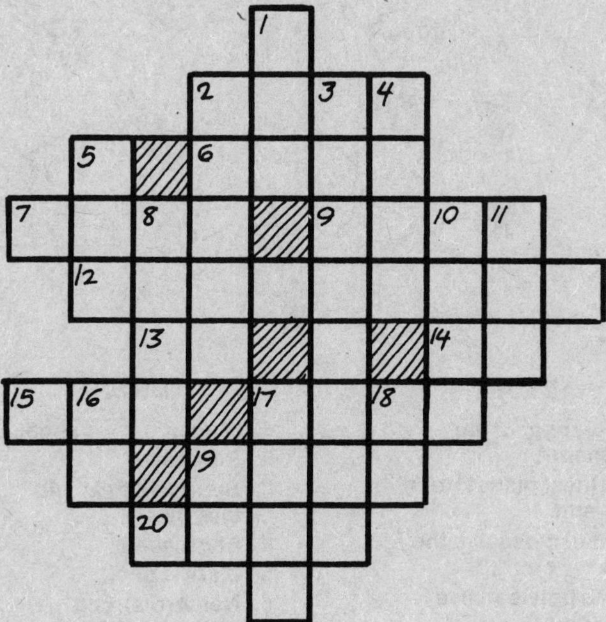
1
2
3
4
5
6
7
8
9
10
11
12
13
14
15
16
17
18
19
20

Heavenly Bodies

ACROSS

1. Beginning of the alphabet.
5. Farthest planet from the sun.
6. Planet closest to the sun: __erc__ry.
7. Area between two buildings.
9. "____ for the money . . ."
10. Grows in a pod.
12. Stanley: nickname.
13. Not close.
14. North Carolina: Abbr.
16. Planet closest in size to earth.
20. School in England.
21. Capital of Italy.

DOWN

1. Ginger _____; soda.
2. Purchase.
3. Source of heat and energy.
4. Engrossed.
5. Mars is one.
6. Neil Armstrong walked on it.
8. Depart.
11. Owns.
12. Support for a flower.
13. Amusement.
17. Negative.
19. Company: Abbr.

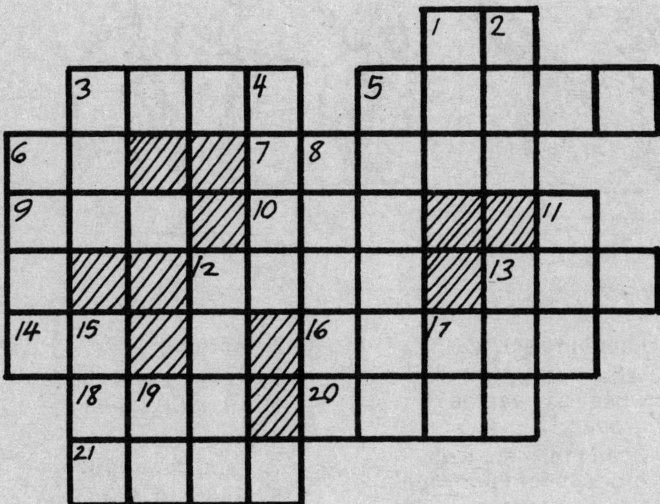
1
2
3
4
5
6
7
8
9
10
11
12
13
14
15
16
17
18
19
20
21

Potpourri

ACROSS

1. Laughing sound.
3. What a cloud is called when it is near the ground.
6. Food that mammals produce for their young.
9. Steamship: Abbr.
11. Belonging to me.
12. Year: Abbr.
13. Very, very warm.
15. South America: Abbr.
16. District attorney: Abbr.
17. Single.
19. Mother.
20. Toward.
22. Kentucky: Abbr.
26. Musical note.

DOWN

2. Morning: Abbr.
3. Buzzing insect.
4. All right.
5. Kind of tree.
7. I am: contraction.
8. Railroad: Abbr.
12. A sharp pull.
14. _____ra-ra-boom-tee-ay.
15. Therefore.
19. Mine.
20. Soft metal.
21. Either.
23. Georgia: Abbr.
24. Lieutenant: Abbr.

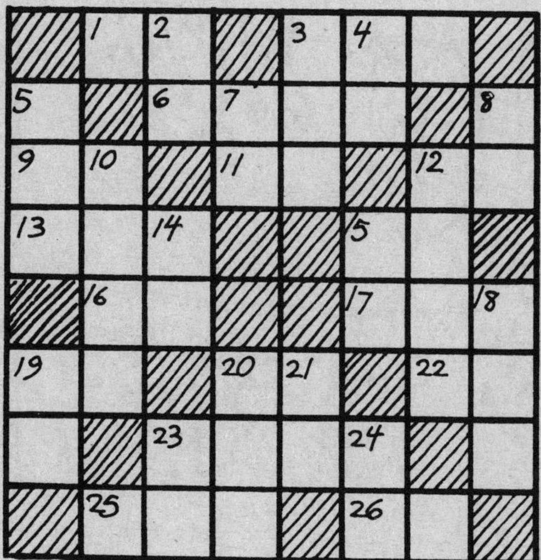
1 2 3 4
5 6 7 8
9 10 11 12
13 14 15
16 17 18
19 20 21 22
23 24
25 26

Clothesline

ACROSS

2. Boy's name.
4. Thick jelly.
7. Place for garbage.
8. Long, long time.
9. Grown-up boy.
10. Coin substitute; a symbol.
14. Weight: Abbr.
15. Louisiana: Abbr.
17. Remedy.
18. "Honest ____" Lincoln.

DOWN

1. Person from Rome.
2. Asian country.
3. Short letter.
7. Boy's hat.
10. Something to use after a bath.
11. Opposite of *in.*
12. Snake like fish.
13. ____ jeans; a color.
16. Gorilla.

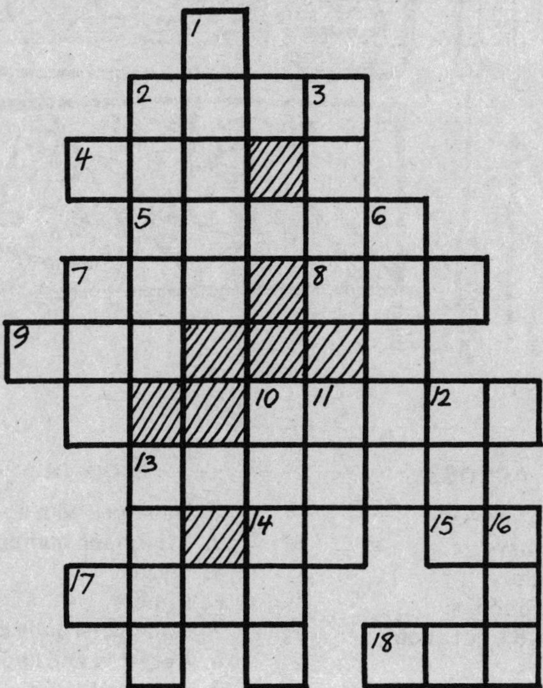
1
2
3
4
5
6
7
8
9
10
11
12
13
14
15
16
17
18

In the Refrigerator

ACROSS

8. _____ cream.
9. Not there.
10. Ganders.
11. Approaches.
13. Baited trap; decoy.
15. Some.
16. "___ say can you see . . ."
18. A unit of power in a light bulb.
19. Sheep talk.
20. Old MacDonald had one.

DOWN

1. Delicious with eggs.
3. 51: Roman numerals.
4. Myself.
6. Eithers.
7. Sound of a baby chick.
10. Very thin and haggard.
12. Filled with joy.
14. Be in debt.
16. Paddle
17. Meat from a hog.
19. Strained fruit: _ _by food.

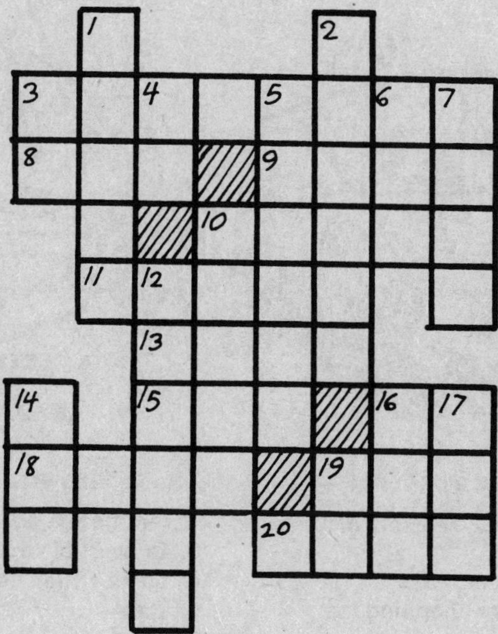
1
2
3
4
5
6
7
8
9
10
11
12
13
14
15
16
17
18
19
20

Away We Go!

ACROSS

2. Pretend; segment of a play.
8. See eye-to-eye.
9. Tool for chopping wood.
10. What hens lay.
12. Took a chance; gambled.
14. Contraction of *I am*.
18. That is *(id est)*: Abbr.
19. Elevated railroad: Abbr.
20. _____, tac, toe.
21. Island.

DOWN

1. Flat-bottomed boats.
3. Convertible or sedan.
4. Make a knot; neckwear.
5. Cab.
6. Used for sewing.
7. Locomotives.
9. Native of Arabia.
11. Sniff; give off an odor.
13. Long, narrative poem.
17. Street or saint: Abbr.

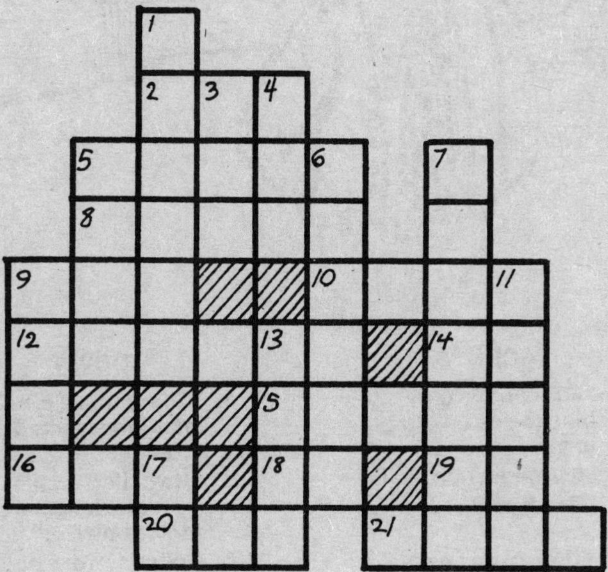

Mother Goose Special

ACROSS

2. "Four and twenty blackbirds baked in a _____ . . ."
4. 56: Roman numerals.
6. "Baa Baa Black _______ . . ."
8. "There was an old woman who lived in a _______ . . ."
9. Boy's name.
10. Speedy.
12. Paintings or sculpture.
13. Bachelor of Arts: Abbr.
15. To sample food.
16. Fuss; bother; much _____ about nothing.
18. "Along came a _______ who sat down beside her . . ."

DOWN

1. "There was a crooked man, who walked a crooked _______ . . ."
2. "He called for his _____ and he called for his bowl . . ."
6. Couches; love seats.
7. "The Queen of _______ she made some tarts . . ."
8. Chair, bench or stool.
11. Stair; put one foot forward.
13. ". . . when she was _______, she was horrid . . ."
14. Lemon _ _ _; summer drink.
17. Either.

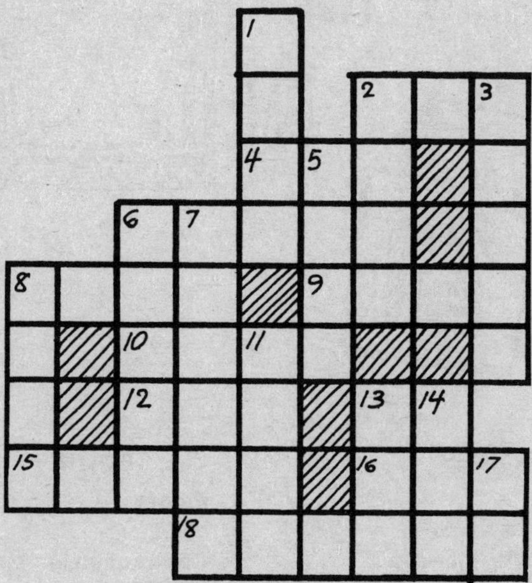
1 2 3 4 5 6 7 8 9 10 11 12 13 14 15 16 17 18

Squares

ACROSS

6. Ocean.
7. Beasts of burden.
9. Part of sleep cycle; Rapid Eye Movement: Abbr.
11. Cast a ballot.
13. Cubes with dots, used in some games.
15. Ajar; not shut.
16. A kind of bread.
17. Loud, irritating sound.
18. Wager.

DOWN

1. Fibber.
3. Us.
5. Contraction for *we have.*
6. Timid; bashful.
8. Not yes.
10. Garden where Adam and Eve lived.
12. Attempt.
14. Spider's lair.
15. Cereal grain; horse food.
16. Bright color.

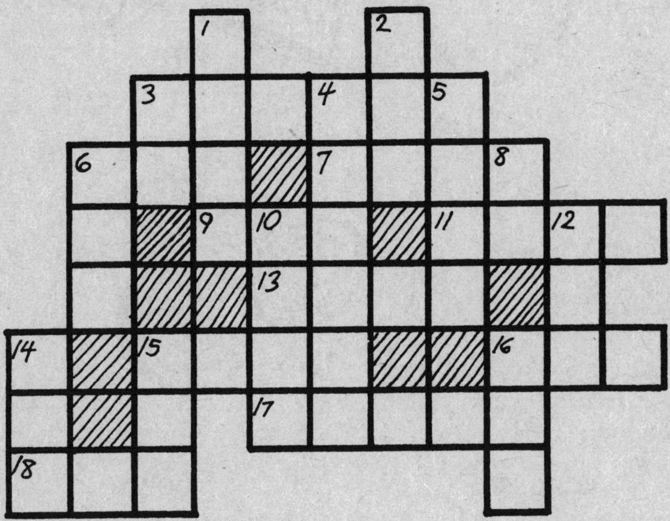

Circles

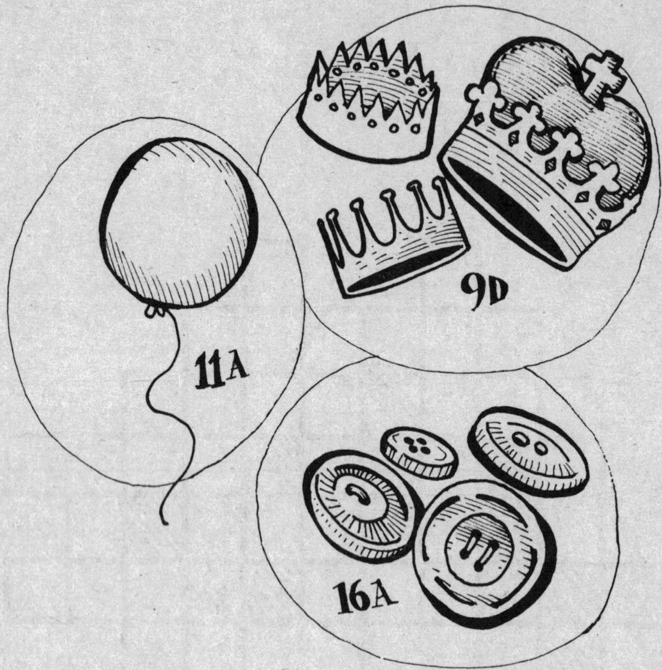

ACROSS

1. Long-playing record (short name).
3. Part of the mouth.
6. Shut the door hard.
7. "... Three men ___ ___ tub ..."
8. Sunburn; light brown.
9. Penny.
10. Renown.
15. Contraction for *will not.*
18. Male child.
19. Place where fabric is joined.

DOWN

1. Camel's relative.
2. Section of a wood wall.
3. An untruth.
4. Country hotel.
5. To tap lightly.
6. Stick with a knife.
12. Tardy.
13. Between your eyes.
14. Tiny particle.
16. Little ___ Peep.
17. Prefix meaning *not.*

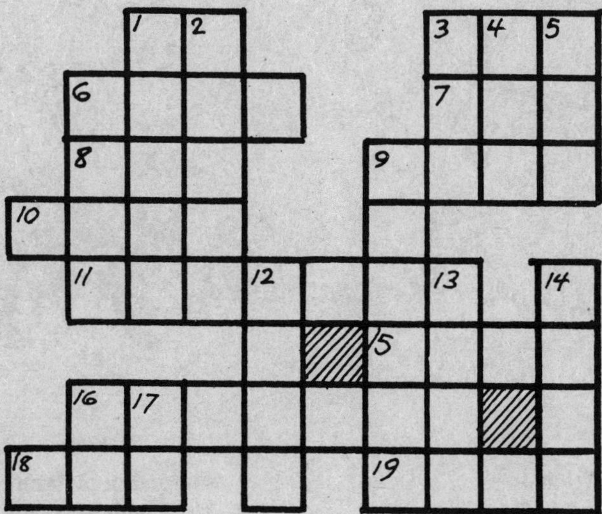

Halloween

ACROSS

8. "Trick or ______."
9. Yes, in Spanish.
10. Something ships throw overboard.
13. Couch; love seat.
15. To be sick; to be _ _ _ing.
16. Something to take a bath in.
19. He fiddled while Rome burned.
20. South America: Abbr.
21. A long time ____.

DOWN

1. Almond or pistachio.
3. Worn with a blouse.
5. ___ and Mrs.
6. Grows in a pod.
7. Animal with a pouch.
9. Distress signal.
11. Owl sound.
13. To chirp or twitter, as a bird.
14. Butter substitute.
17. Uncle Sam's country.

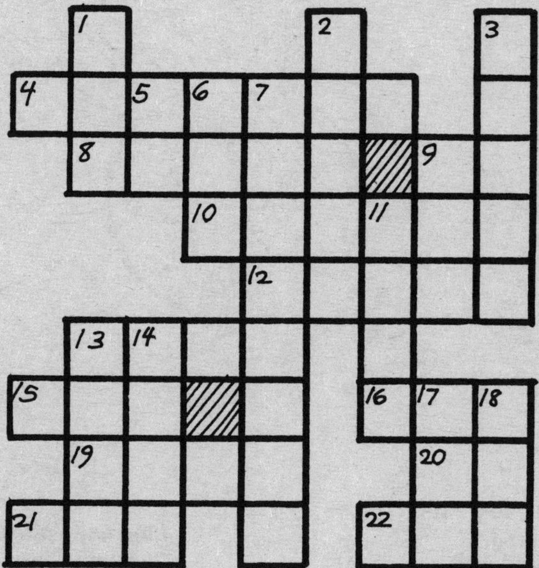

Communications

ACROSS

4. Soft, felt hats.
7. Existed.
10. Reading material; novels.
13. Boy's name.
15. Painting or drawing.
17. Window glass.
18. A path, road, or street..

DOWN

2. Cinema; picture show.
5. Division: Abbr.
6. Residence: Abbr.
9. Hit with open hand.
10. Prohibit.
11. Wood-cutting tool.
12. Pigpen.
14. Louisiana: Abbr.
16. Sun God of ancient Egypt.

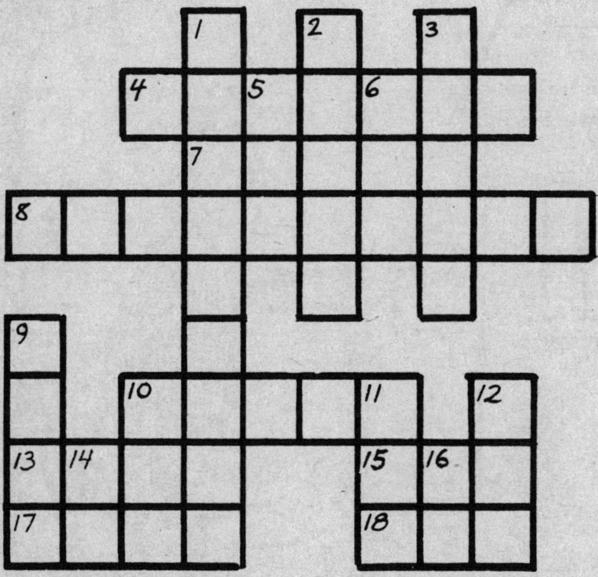

In the Garden

1
2
3
4
5
6

Pass the Fruit

ACROSS

9. Seed inside a peach.
10. Nothing.
11. Dried plum.
12. Mother.
13. Ran from danger.
14. One; lone.
16. Ganders.
17. Yellowish-red tropical fruit.

DOWN

1. Hat worn by men from Turkey.
4. Cars have four.
5. Musical composition.
6. Yellow citrus fruit.
7. We drink its juice.
8. Negative answer.
13. Not many.

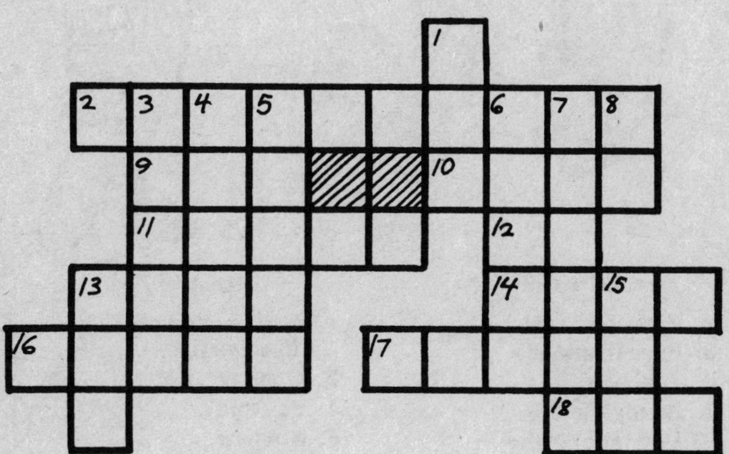

Numbers

ACROSS

1. Part of a circle.
3. Even number.
6. That boy.
7. Ready! Set! ____!
9. 12th letter in the alphabet.
10. Window glass.
12. Act.
13. Dine.
17. __-so (fair).
19. Slightly sour.
22. Morning.
24. Doctor: Abbr.
25. Toward.
26. Roman numeral X.
27. Half a dozen.

DOWN

1. Exclamation of discovery.
2. Musical note.
4. You and I.
5. Not new.
7. Georgia: Abbr.
8. Single.
10. __ __ __ __ hole, (ship's window).
11. Opposite of West.
12. District attorney: Abbr.
14. I'm going ___ the store.
16. Angry.
18. Not skinny.
20. Railroad: Abbr.
23. Myself.
25. Musical note.

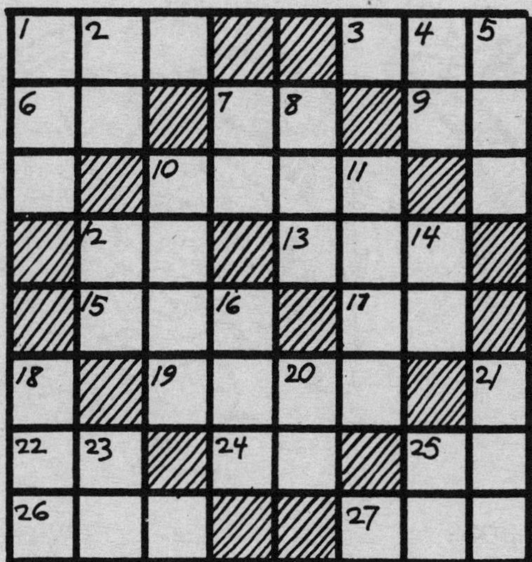

Busy Bones

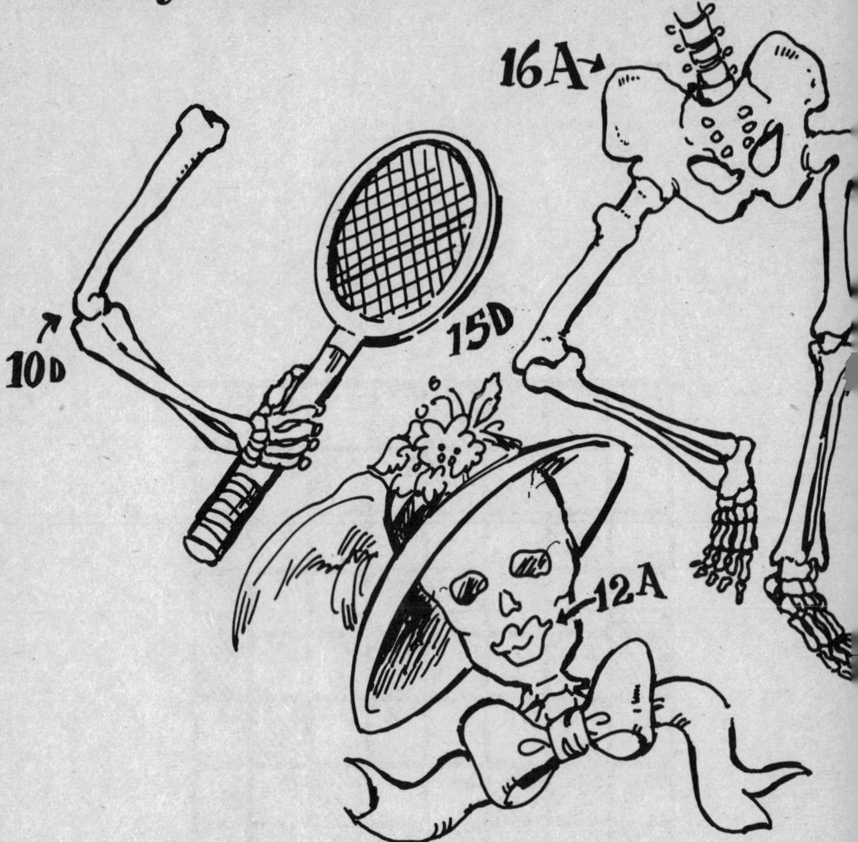

ACROSS

1. Landslide.
7. Mother.
8. Less than two.
9. Prizefighters.
11. Shipped.
13. Obtained.
17. Opposite of yes.
18. Not you.
19. ________ is me!
20. ________ of smell; one of five.

DOWN

1. Morning: Abbr.
2. Enclosed truck.
3. Part of ear.
4. Soon; presently.
5. Not *this* time (two words).
6. She.

14. Not closed.

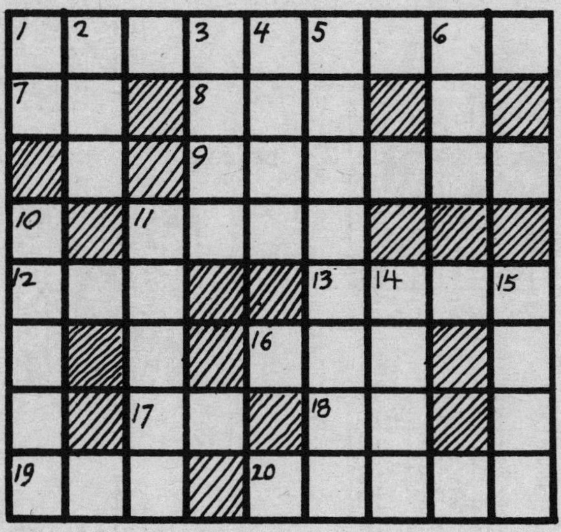

Answers

page 3

page 4

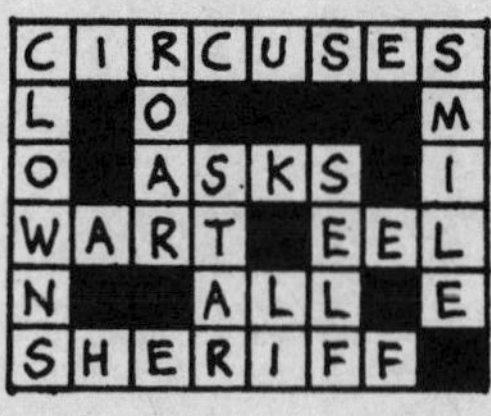

page 6

page 8

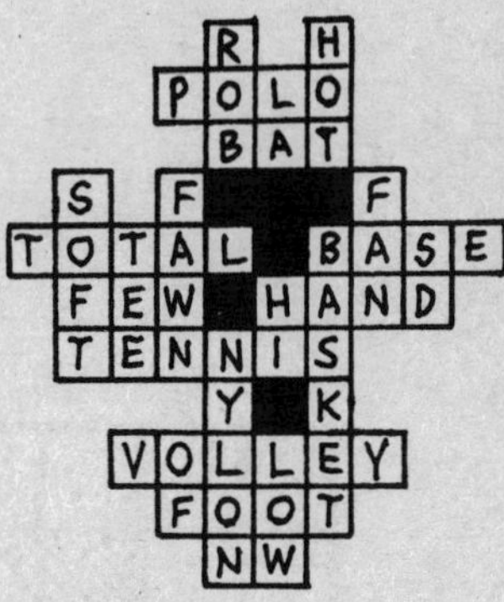

page 10

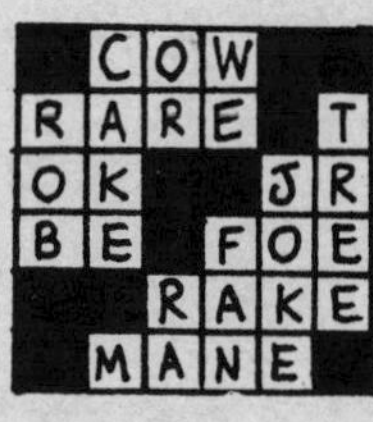

page 12

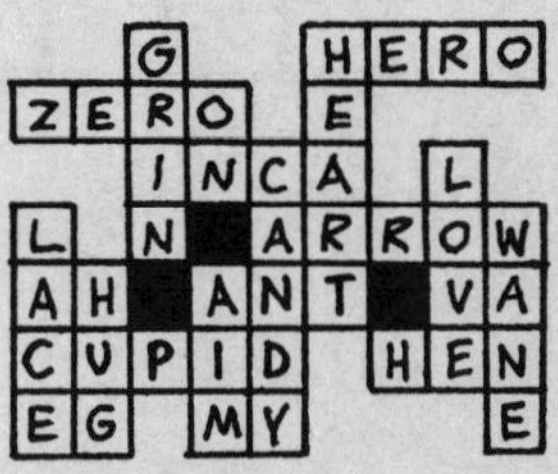

page 14

page 16

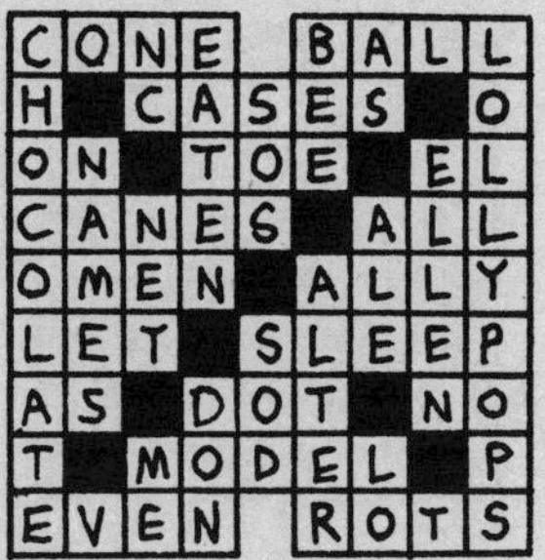

page 18

page 20

page 22

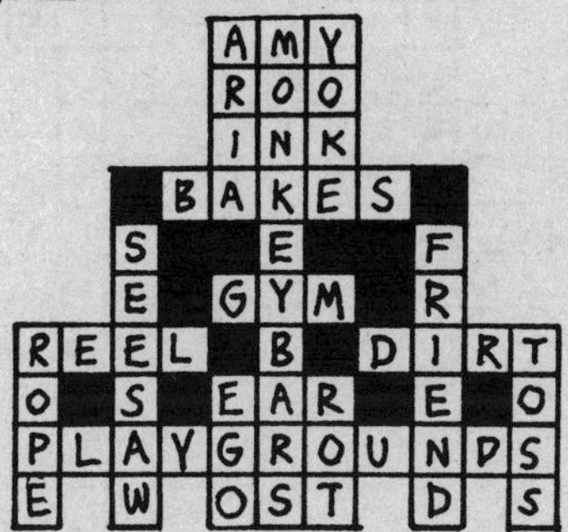

page 24

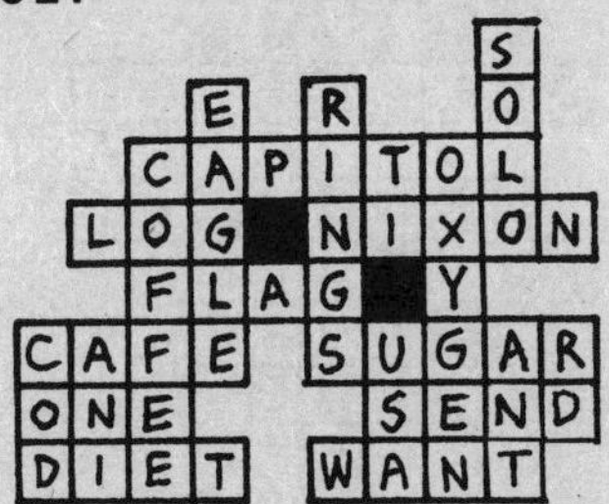

page 26

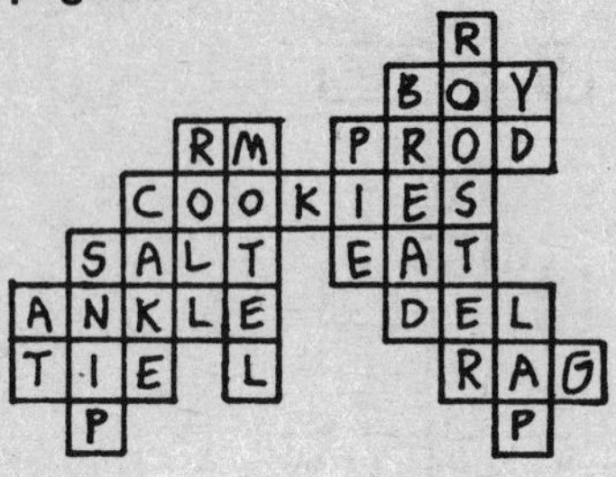

page 28

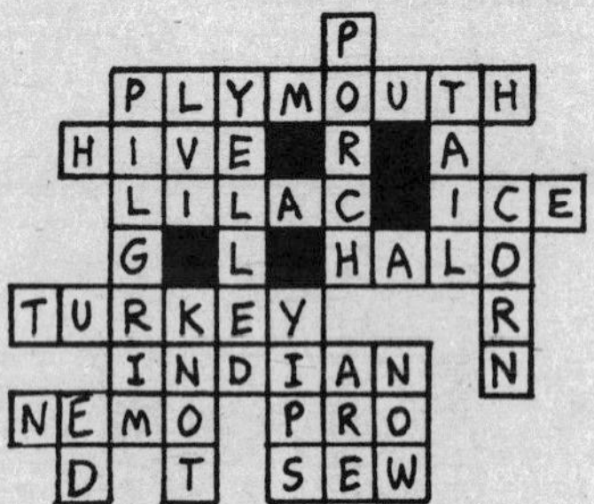

page 30

page 32

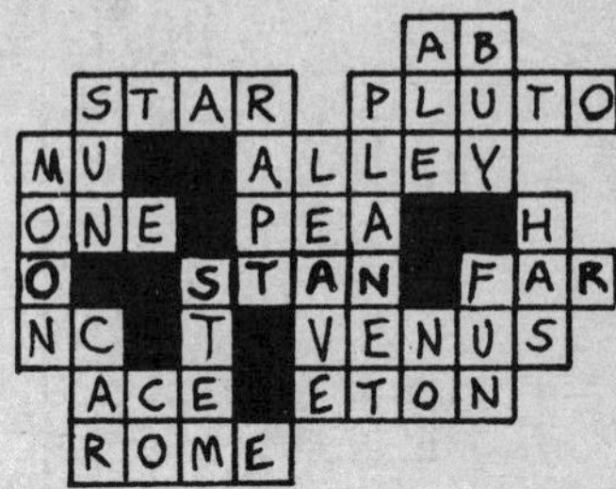

page 34

page 36

page 38

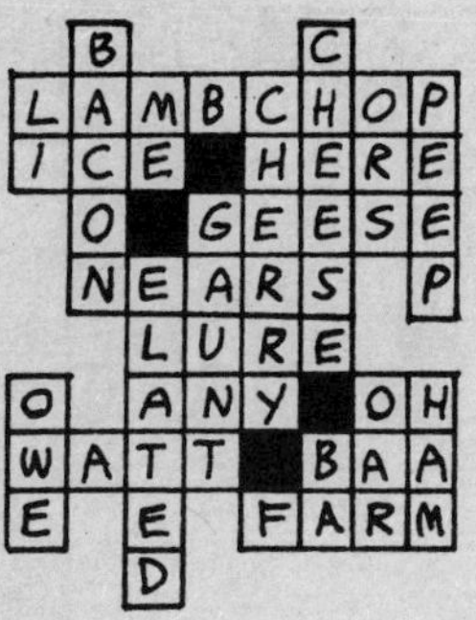

page 40

page 42

page 44

page 46

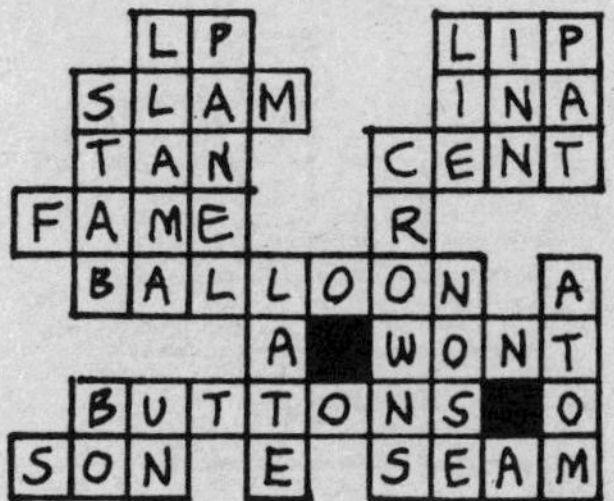

page 48

page 50

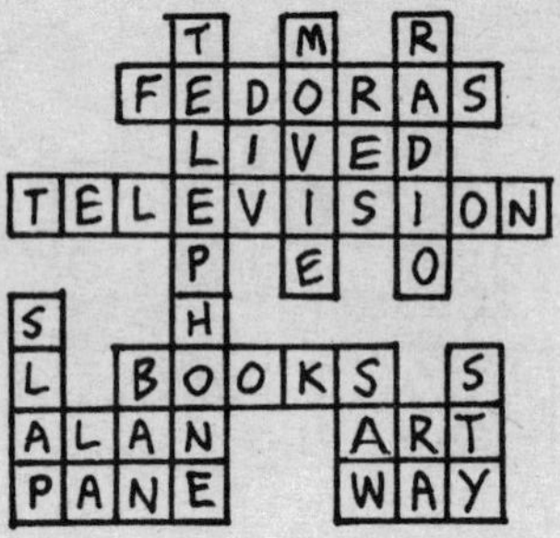

page 56

page 52

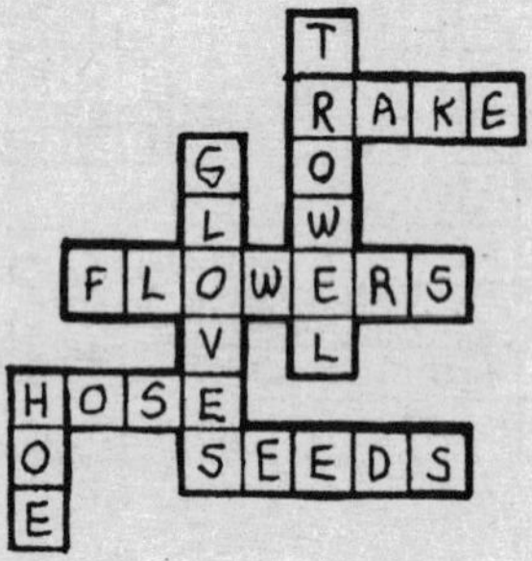

page 58

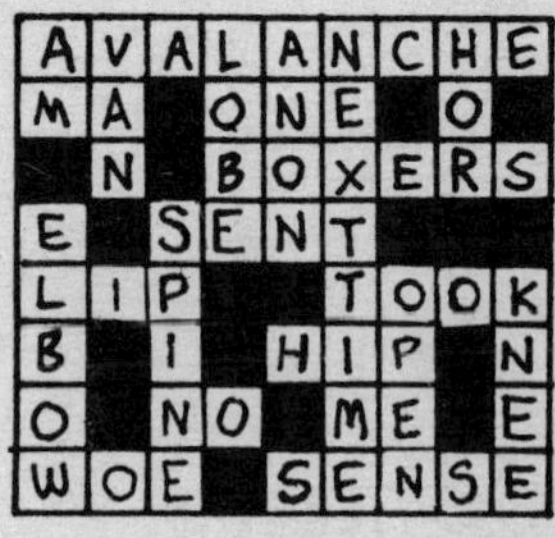

page 54

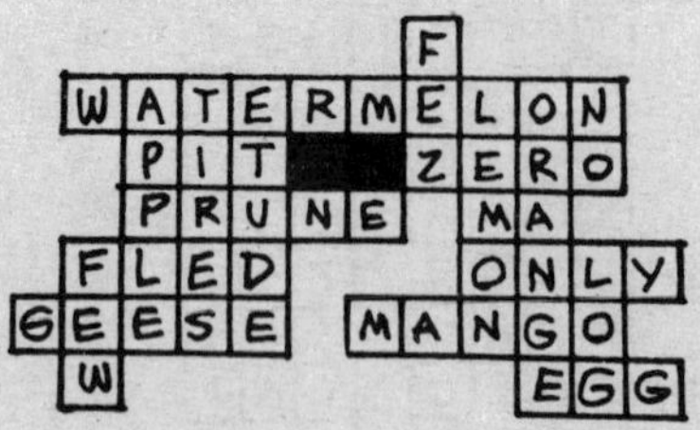